SKETCHES OF THE
SOUTHSIDE

Lorette E. Roberts

BLACKSMITH BOOKS

SKETCHES OF THE SOUTHSIDE

ISBN 978-988-13764-7-3

First published as *Sketches of Stanley*
www.loretteroberts.com
The moral right of the Author has been asserted.

Published by Blacksmith Books
Unit 26, 19/F, Block B, Wah Lok Industrial Centre,
37-41 Shan Mei Street, Fo Tan, Hong Kong
Tel: (+852) 2877 7899
www.blacksmithbooks.com

Chinese translations by Wee Kek Koon

Deck Chairs Relaxing — Shek O Beach.

FOREWORD

I have to confess up front to being at least partly responsible for encouraging Lorette to produce a book on the Southside of Hong Kong Island. At the outset she didn't know the area beyond occasional visits to dine out or hike in the hills. But as I watched Lorette undertake her exploration, reconnaissance and research, I saw her increasing excitement about the project, the diversity of the area and all the unexpected things she found, until eventually I heard the familiar refrain: "But I'm never going to fit everything I want in the book…"

My family and I live among the people and places Lorette has drawn and painted – her book reminds us of the beauty and variety of this part of Hong Kong. With her attention to detail and inquisitive nature, she has captured, in her own inimitable style, everything from temples to monasteries; dai pai dong to exclusive private clubs; sailors, surfers, swimmers, hikers, dragon boat paddlers and mini rugby players; sharks at Ocean Park, lobsters at Cape D'Aguilar and huge spiders in Tai Tam country park.

Lorette's earlier books have been hugely popular – *Sketches of the Southside* will undoubtedly be just as successful. Sit back, turn the pages and sink into Lorette's world as she takes you on a new and revealing trip from Aberdeen to Shek O. What a wonderful advertisement for the Southside!

Christopher Bailey
Picture This Gallery

DEDICATION

This sketchbook is for Jean, my mother-in-law, and Jean, my friend from North California. Both have an indefatigable spirit and a wicked sense of humour.

ACKNOWLEDGEMENTS

WOW, Ruby, Jenny Day, Gien Viernes, Carole Carlin, Lorna Tesoy, Pete Spurrier, Roger Nissim, Bill Greaves, Jason Wordie, Alissia Roberts, Douglas, Tina and Guy Roberts, Lynne Campbell, Wee Kek Koon, Leo Kwok, Bettina Proessdorf, Carolynne Pike, W. Don Chow, Anne Marden, Pamela and Christopher Bailey, Amelia Roberts, Robert Dale, Guy Nowell, Rose Cheng and all those who have unwittingly crept into my sketches or have contributed to making this such a lively project.

Also to Kaman Ho at Ocean Park, Annie Chan from The Repulse Bay, Gregory De'eb at the Crown Wine Cellars, Gray Williams from the Swire Institute of Marine Science, Department of Ecology and Biodiversity, HKU and Stephen Davies from the Hong Kong Maritime Museum for their time and inside knowledge!

Thanks for your help with this book; either with information, inspiration or invitations to lunch.

Pencil & Wash —

The "Umbrella-Chair?" Ladies. Shek O beach —

JUST TO SAY...

That anyone who has left the city and tunnelled through to Aberdeen, then onto Stanley and the Southside of Hong Kong Island, knows that they have reached a tourist paradise; shopping, restaurants, shopping, dragon boats, more shopping and, for the energetic, water sports and hiking. I have to agree, but over the past few months of exploring, plus several notebooks and pencils later, I found a much greater legacy. Not only memories of war but history of earlier times: rock carvings, tales of pirates, old homes and even older temples, turn of the century engineering and some mysteries too (who were Mills and Chung?)

I marvel that only a hundred years ago, people travelled to Deep Water Bay for a round of golf by boat or on horseback (dedication indeed!) I was delighted by the traditional villages; intrigued by the homes painted in rainbow colours; amazed by the multiplicity of pot plants in obscure places; amused to see scarecrows; and of course, refreshed in Stanley!

This eclectic collection of sketches is my personal choice (my snails are hidden everywhere). I hope it stirs sunny memories for you but if, inadvertently, I have left out your absolute favourite place, there is a page at the back for your own sketches!

Lorette x

The Golden Dragon, at the Entrance —

歡迎光臨
WELCOME
ようこそ
어서오십시오

Sketched at the Jumbo floating Restaurant — Here are just 10 of the multiplicity of Painted - mosaic - modelled - Carved - Gilded - Stencilled & engraved Dragons* that decorate this very big place. *I did not see a single Elephant!

Two tourist Couples on the Dragon Throne

All "Dolled up" as a Chinese noble-woman, in years past —

CHOP STICK COVER

珍寶王國

After Dinner—
A Backwards
glance at the
Jumbo—

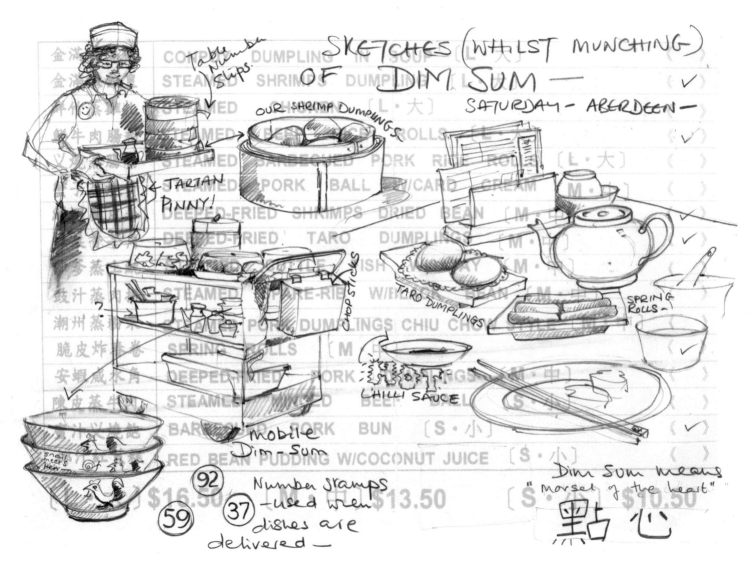

An Elderly fish market worker having her "Elevenses"

A Wild Pomegranate Tree by the Bus Depot. along with several butterflies — (+ lots of boats!)

Walking along Aberdeen Promenade & Praya Road — after enjoying Dim Sum

香潤
記榮
14
8

Wood Seafood Vats High above, soon to be winched into a lorry —

About ±4m High —

Time piece as sculpture & ...

...this Could be a piece of Installation ART.

By the steps of the sampan

財祖手
開工大吉
上洛平發
順水

Two GAUDY plastic fish and several sun-bleached couplets wish sampan travellers 'Bon Voyage' & peaceful Cross-Harbour Travels —

ABERDEEN WHOLESALE FISH MARKET
香港仔魚類批發市場

小心
車輛出入

Very
early on a
Saturday morning-

Despatch Dockets

Electric cable

One of
many
Weigh
Stations.

Very small wholesale order or his packed lunch?

NUMEROUS
ENORMOUS
DELIVERY
TRUCKS

This is
a hose -
not an
escaping
Eel -

WOT
no
wellies?

MIND YOUR HEAD 小心石裡頭

343A

34

Dog Watch?

Old Boat

Living and Working in
Aberdeen Harbour
香港仔灣之民情風貌

Proud Prows

桂記船廠 5521G

Smith yard
Repair yard

Bird's Eye
View from the
Peak Road
山頂道鳥瞰

Morning in
Aberdeen Harbour
香港仔灣

Wardrobe, larder and office sampan style!

A Sampan
Ride
剩生帆船

"Sampan" translates
as "Three boards" —
ie. A simple boat.
Traditionally, they
were operated
by women.

Skilled sampan skipper.

☆ N.B!
Dear Tourists — do
NOT all sit on one side
of a sampan!!

O.1 Pen
+ Sepia
& Paynes
Grey.

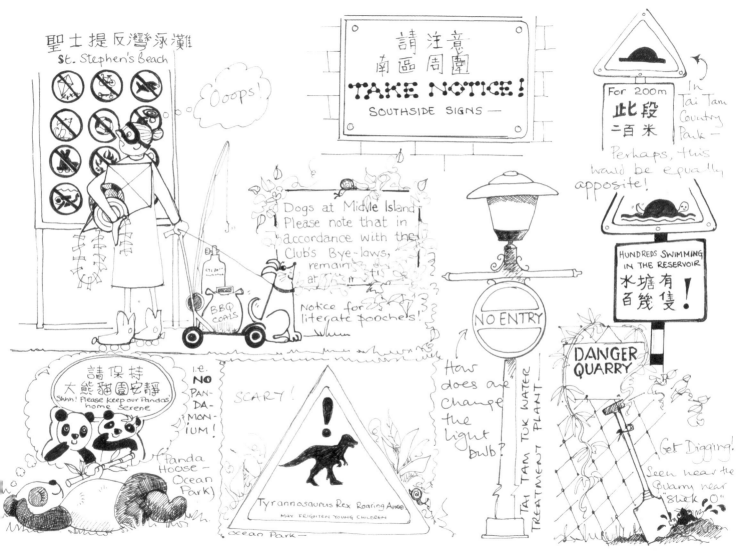

IN THE AVIARY—

PANDA
HABITAT—

A 'Brush' with
Residents at
Ocean Park—

GOLDFISH
PAGODA

SEA DRAGON

ATOLL
REEF

SEA HORSE.

Dolphin in
Ocean Theatre.

"Pink"

SHARK TUNNEL

SEALS IN
PACIFIC
PIER —

ATOLL REEF

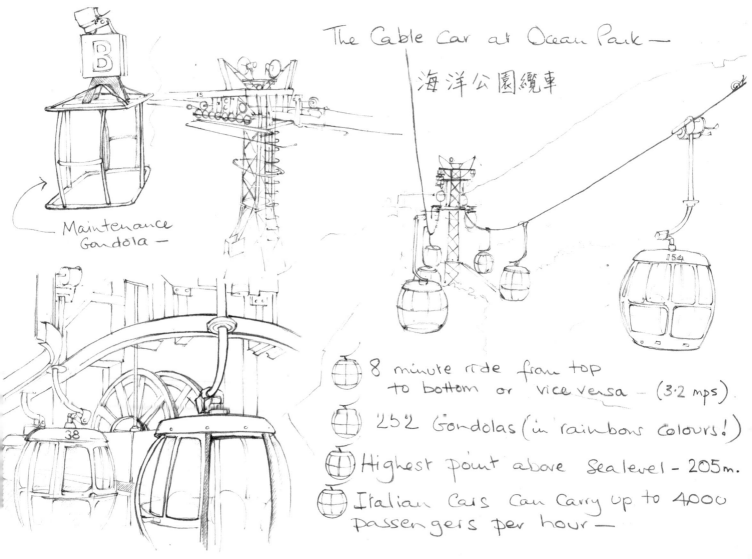

The Cable Car at Ocean Park —

海洋公園纜車

Maintenance Gondola —

8 minute ride from top
to bottom or vice versa — (3.2 mps)

252 Gondolas (in rainbow colours!)

Highest point above Sea level - 205m.

Italian Cars can carry up to 4000
passengers per hour —

The Dragon Roller
Coaster — 842 m. long track

The Eagle Ride —
31m. High — 28 gondolas
(56 people)

The Ferris Wheel
27m. High — 18 gondolas
(108 people enjoying the view)

The Abyss Turbo Drop —
62m. High Tower — The fall lasts a few
seconds, with an initial force of -1G
experienced by the passengers —

Headland Rides — in
full swing — from the
Ocean Theatre —

GARDENS 花園

Ocean Park's own Floral Dinosaur (or Florasaur?)

LONGINES

The Repulse Bay Floral Clock — (5 m. in diameter) — was made by Longines and installed at The Repulse Bay Hotel in 1976 — It was returned to the site after the Renovations were completed.

The Hanging Gardens of Tai Tam —

71752A

The Floating Garden of Aberdeen —

The Hanging Garden of Wang Chuk Hang San Wai

Village Houses......
&..... GARDENS
村屋....
及花園

"Scarecrows" —
Uniquely Hong-Kong Style!

A martyr
to the
Agricultural
Cause?

Last Year's
Decorations
recycled—

✱ It is when you notice the Old Ocean Park logo on the hillside behind the village roofs, that you realise that Wong Chuk Hang San Wai is only a couple of minutes from Aberdeen Tunnel — not deep in the New Territories —

The newly renovated Village House with Wonderful plaster decorations was probably built in 1890 by a relative of Shouson Chow — who gave his name to SHOUSON Hill —

Little Inhabitant of Upper Street peeping at me!

What an AMAZING Water Pipe —

A very fishy Roof drain —

WONG CHUK HANG

黄竹坑

probably the oldest village in Hong Kong — ALOE ALOE?

This is the village where the old lady told me that I should be sketching the big houses in Shouson Hill — I wanted to tell her that "Beauty was in the eye of the beholder" — & that I was happy right where I was! ✍

HAT

Southside's Ancient Rock Carvings (Petroglyphs!)
古代石刻

How strange to copy lichen-covered
carvings done so very long
ago —
The more
you look,
the more you
discern —

Just outside Aberdeen —
Leave the busy, trafficky Road,
Turn left at the
        Building site,
Climb past the
        High-Rises,
the path is overgrown;
'But there is a ruiled
        Walkway —
You can not miss the rock
        by the little Ravine —
Here someone left a message;
Thousands of years ago —

At Big Wave
Bay —

(Looking at this
reminded me to
"phone home!" —)

STANLEY Military Cemetery—

☀ Metal Door

Legacies of WWII
第二世界大戰的遺物

Concealed in
Undergrowth—
Seaview Promenade.

The Pill-
box on the
D'Aguilar
Peninsula
(two'
binoculars)

mural with Vine motifs —

In what was once the Central Ordnance (munitions) Depot, Crown Wine Cellars utilize the remaining 8 of the original 24 underground bunkers built in the 1930s by the British Military — The New conservatory leads two' to Bunkers approx. 20m. below ground with 2m. thick walls — — Ideal for the storage of wine!

This room was used for the storage of Hand-grenades + has solid reinforced walls —

This 12m. passage is designed in a Zig-Zag formation to deflect potential blast waves —

4B

B

Crown Wine Cellars —
Shouson Hill —
Hong Kong —

* One of two metal doors leading into a bunker —

The Aberdeen Marina Club —

1983 —

V.R.C.

Canopy over Entrance to The Victoria Recreation Club, Deep Water Bay.

STANLEY Fishermen's Recreation Club —

The Aberdeen Boat Club — Established in 1967 —

The Hong Kong Golf Club first built a club House in Deep Water Bay in 1898 —

The American Club — Tai Tam (1980s)

So many Windows!

café Tapas **Uno**

DEEP WATER BAY〜

深水

灣

COCOCABANA

WARNING SIGNALS.
FOR SWIMMERS &
WATER SPORTSMEN.

LIFEGUARD IN ATTENDANCE.

SHARK IN THE VICINITY

SWIMMING UNSAFE. DO NOT ENTER WATER.

FIRST AID STATION.

Mills & Chung Path
茆鍾徑
∘∘ c. late 1980's ∘∘

- Built as part of a
Hong Kong Electric project
Mills & Chung
PATH was
named after its
proponents ——

Road to Aberdeen Tunnel

VICTORIA
Recreation
Club.

V
R
C

CANOES.

Monday Morning!
6.45 AM   29°C

Deep Water Bay —
深水灣

The beach is swarming
with enthusiasts —
doing Tai Chi, stretching,
jogging, splashing, swimming —
laughing, shrieking —
radio blaring —
Teenagers?
Well yes, once, but now
Septo- and Octogenarians
Enjoy themselves before
they have their Dim Sum!

A Spectrum of Swim Caps!
七彩泳帽

好嘢!   咪!

dumped where hunky
later hang-out!!

Commodious
belongings are
life guards will

FERRIES

渡輪

The Po Toi Ferry leaving St Stephen's Beach

120708

Fast 'ferry' from To Tei Wan Tsuen (Buy the ticket at to Stanley) and Tai Tam Tuk — the noodle shop on the Beach!)

& After a long Sunday BBQ, the ferry from Middle Island

RHKYC M71

往南丫島
(模達灣·索罟灣)
碼頭

TO LAMMA ISLAND
(MO TAT WAN SOK KWU WAN)
PIER

全記渡有限公司
CHUEN KEE FERRY LTD

往
蒲苔
HA

STRANGE handrail

Nice way to travel home at the end of a long day

Racing "Optimists" —
(flat bottomed, hard-chine, pram-bow 7'6½ ins x 3'8" wide — 77 lbs. in weight).

香港遊艇會
熨波洲

The Royal Hong Kong Yacht Club — Middle Island

The first recorded sailing/ rowing races were in 1937. Middle Island had a "mat shed" (which succumbed to a typhoon) & was replaced by a brick built Club House.

ROYAL HONG KONG YACHT CLUB
MIDDLE ISLAND
香港遊艇會
熨波洲

Aged
Aippy
Assistant

They are more
likely to get
"Wet feet" than
"Cold feet"

SHEKO

- MIDDLE ISLAND -

CUTE

SHEKO
Dad to the
Rescue!

— Anxious Pet Owner — He will be in Deep Water if he doesn't take more notice of his girl friend —

Deep Water Bay —

Sunday Morning Repulse Bay — [Gossip Column]

ON The Beach —

海灘上

Middle Island beach —

Tunnel Excavation in Progress — (A bit Optimistic!)

The SHELL O EXPRESS.

The Best thing about Sketching on the Beach: Hands & feet are often hidden in the Sand!

~Around The Repulse Bay~

影灣園內外

This means "flight of the Phoenix"

Very privileged!!!

Aerial View of
Repulse Bay

淺水灣鳥瞰

Through the little wrought iron gate —

The Repulse Bay Nursery —

Plaster Cornice

Decorative Features in the Bamboo Bar —

Window Hinge —

Quick Sketches around

THE VERANDAH RESTAURANT

Brass Door Hinge

Brass Bolt.

Part of The Repulse Bay Complex (built in late 1980s) has replica door furniture harking back to the days of the old Repulse Bay Hotel (1920 - 1982).

The Repulse Bay

Noodle Breakfast al fresco —

Tiny Waterfall

UBIQUITOUS Red Plastic Bucket!

麗海堤岸路

Pencil & wash — Sketches whilst wandering around.. (7am)

Fishing for Breakfast —

Evocative vignette —

SEAVIEW PROMENADE

Lots of Dog Walkers — (This one is still little even when stretching!)

Tally: 9 Labradors/Retrievers
11 fluffy little dogs —
1 Dalmation —
1 Dog of unknown origin*
(+ a crafty cat or two!).

Bracket on Old building on Beach Road —

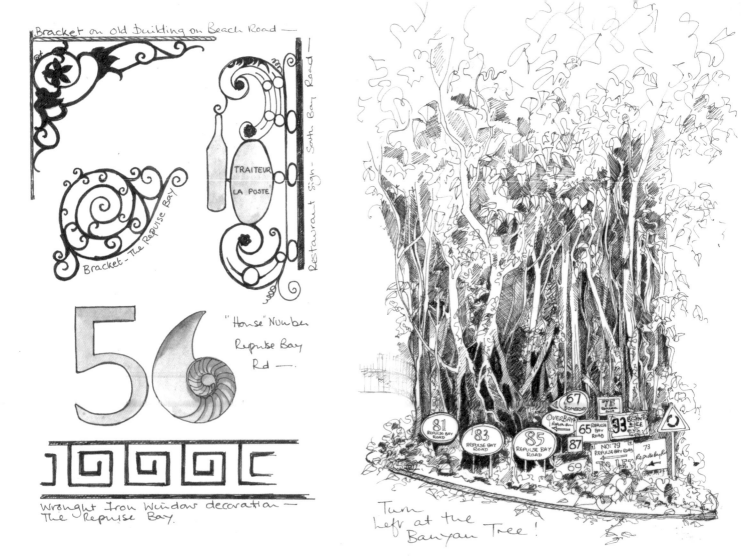

TRAITEUR
LA POSTE

Restaurant Sign - South Bay Road

Bracket - The Repulse Bay

"House" Number
Repulse Bay
Rd —

56

Wrought Iron Window decoration —
The Repulse Bay.

81 REPULSE BAY ROAD
83 REPULSE BAY ROAD
85 REPULSE BAY ROAD
67 SOMERSET
7E SOMERSET BACK
OverBay REPULSE BAY
65 REPULSE BAY ROAD
93 CRESTVIEW
87
NO 79 REPULSE BAY ROAD
TO LET
73 Repulse Bay
69

Turn
Left at the
Banyan Tree!

"OVERGROWN!

野草丛生

Tall brick chimney at the water — Tai Tam Tuk —
Treatment plant — 35

ADDRESS unknown!

Redundant Chimney in Repulse Bay

One might say it's "Curtains" for this window

Old sign for a village shop — Nam Fung Path — 南記士多 上來右便

Hok Tsui Tsuen — A Different slant on LONG STAY PARKING.

天后像

A little visitor rests in the shadow of the Buddha, while her family explore the wonders of the Life Guard Terraces and Tii Hau temple on Repulse Bay Beach — There are statues of Goddesses to be seen and mythical Beasts too!

SQUEAKY CLEAN — Brand New Pink Shoes!

請

In the Terraced gardens on Repulse Bay Beach —

The tallest statue of the Goddess in Hon Kon →

— Phoenix & Dragon —

Decorative tiles

8

MOUNTBATTEN
Youth Recreation Center
Hong Kong Life Guards
South Bay Road

總 拯 香
會 溺 港

hot sea-water but concrete for some reason

南海龍珠

GODDESS OF REPULSE BAY

灣水海南
之神

※ I often wonder how many million little ceramic tiles have been used in Hong Kong —

The massive Dragon Shell from the China Sea - About 2000 Years old !

Stanley's two ancient
Banyan Trees —

It looks a happy home —
— STANLEY —

Famous roadside Temple in Deep Water Bay.

天后古廟

Temple in SHEKO

SOUTHSIDE TEMPLES

A 120 year old "Little Temple" in the centre of Kau Wai Village.

廟宇

The large statue of KWUN YUM overlooking STANLEY.

Watch dog!

The Yellow Temple by the fish farm in LAN NAI WAN TSUEN — (opposite Redhill Peninsula) (over enthusiastic watch dog — so I could not get any closer !!)

Traditional Green tiled roof & red Pillars — overlooking Middle Island.

Like Towns the World over, STANLEY has its share of eclectic architecture — some "native" to the area & some relocated!

The Tai Wong Temple — dedicated to a water God who protects fishing villagers — This familiar little Temple is on STANLEY MAIN ROAD (There is usually a news-stand set up just in front!)

8 Praya or "Alms Houses" — An interconnecting brick terrace-built by the Government in 1950s — overlooking STANLEY Bay — to rehouse eight village families from Wong Ma Kok.

119

善安公所

開千秋兄弟深情

*Restored in the DING WEI YEAR of DAOGUANG Emperor's reign — (1847)

This Stone doorway was the entrance to the village (welfare) Office — now the STANLEY KAIFONG WELFARE ADVANCEMENT ASSOCIATION!!!!

結萬古兄弟大志

THE HONG KONG SEA SCHOOL
中立陸濟海泳浮

* coiled rope details

Feb. 1st 1964

The Hong Kong Sea School — Opened by King BAUDOUIN of BELGIUM

Built 1935 — The Maryknoll mission — 瑪利吉節

This TIEN HOU Temple was built in
(TIN HAU)
the 32 year of CH'IEN LUNG—
(1769)—
The 'Tien Hau' festival is
celebrated on the 23
day of the
3rd Moon—

廣安里同昌大押司昌大押行

Old
Pillars
relocated
to STANLEY
from
Shanghai
Street
then
Races—
around
H.K

— STANLEY INLAND LOT 26—
These numbers and figures
refer to the Lot number — a system
no longer used — a piece of history!

S.I.L.
26
STANLEY MARKET ROAD.

An Ornate Grill
on the Side window
of STANLEY Post Office — the
"GR" incorporated suggests
that the building is at
least 50 years old—

NO: 50, STANLEY Village Rd.
One of the very
few remaining
large
family
homes
built
between
the Wars.

MURRAY HOUSE—
Built in 1844
and located in Central—
It was dismantled in
1982 + Stored. Rebuilt in
STANLEY in 1998 - it now houses the
Hong Kong Maritime Museum—

STANLEY MARKET— Any Time, Any Day !

Matthew Gallery

← accept orders
paint
← PORTRAITS
from
← PHOTOES

龍馬精神

GOOD HEALTH
POWER
LIKE
DRANGON HORSE

SHOP
27店

STANLEY MARKET

Queens 御

19A

COOL!
WOW!

Fancy
feet of
Clay.

LOOK
Beyond
the Racks
of
Cheong Sam and
Tee Shirts —
There is the
Temple!

Busy
Page —
Busy
Market!

Toy Dog
meets real
Toy Dog!

IN STANLEY...

Stanley Restaurant
赤柱餐廳

Little "Ladies who 'lunch"
$30
$30
$20
$30

ChilliN Spice
TEL: 2899 0147

EL CID
Caramar
TEL 2899 0958

CHINESE RESTAURANT –
STANLEY MARKET

The SMUGGLERS INN

$90/$60
$65
$78
$90
$75

CURRY POT

A reminder of STANLEY'S history

Restaurants are sprouting up EVERYWHERE!

FISH 'N' CHIPS
$7
$68
$72

Detail of the door at LUCY'S

Balustrade detail –

Masala/Korma/Garlic/Madras
Bombay Fish Curry
Chicken Masala/Korma/Butter/Madras
Lamb C "BEACHES"
daloo (very spicy)

VEGETABLES

Vegetable
Saag Paneer
Spinach & Co...

Waiting for the Sunday Brunch rush! –
SEAFRONT

Blue Tower Landmark 17. Gobi Aloo (Cau...
The Boathouse Restaurant – ...hani (Black Lentils)   SAIGON & SUKHOTHAI Restaurants

$50
MENU FROM THE CURRY POT.

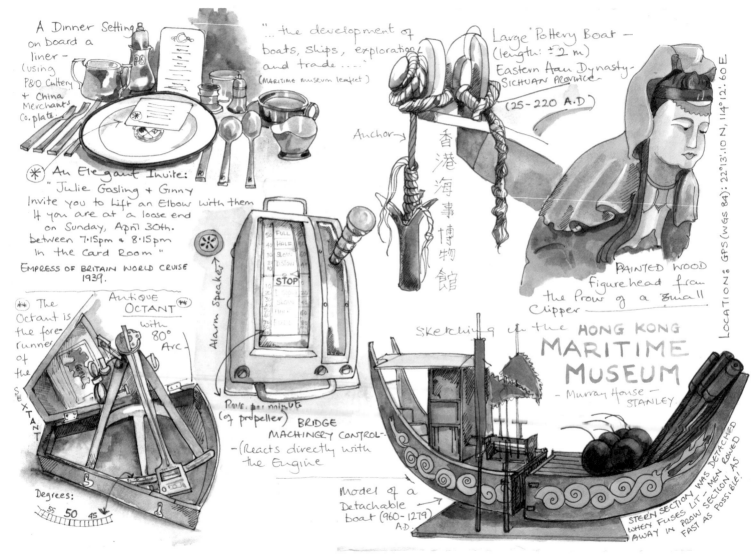

A Dinner Setting on board a liner — (using P&O Cutlery + China Merchants Co. plate)

"... the development of boats, ships, exploration and trade ...."
(Maritime museum leaflet)

Large 'Pottery Boat' — (length: ±2 m) Eastern Han Dynasty- Sichuan Province (25-220 A.D)

Anchor→

香港海事博物館

⊛ An Elegant Invite:
"Julie Gasling & Ginny invite you to Lift an Elbow with them if you are at a loose end on Sunday, April 30th. between 7.15pm & 8.15pm in the Card Room"
Empress of Britain World Cruise 1939.

Painted wood figurehead from the Prow of a small Clipper.

⊛⊛ The Octant is the fore-runner of the Sextant

Antique OCTANT ⊛⊛
with 80° Arc

Alarm Speaker→

FULL
HALF
SLOW
D.SLOW
STOP
D.SLOW
SLOW
HALF
FULL

Sketching in the HONG KONG MARITIME MUSEUM
— Murray House —
STANLEY.

Revs. per minute (of propeller)
BRIDGE MACHINERY CONTROL-
-(Reacts directly with the Engine

Degrees:
55 50 45

Model of a Detachable boat (960-1279) A.D.

Stern section was detached when fuses lit — men rowed away in prow section as fast as possible!

Location: GPS (WGS 84): 22°13'.10 N, 114°12'.60 E

Fancy wrought iron grid on village House fanlight —

sketches for DOORS

← Dead wood Sculpture — NOT A MORIBUND MOGGIE!

門

禧鴻

131

平安是福

富貴由天

New and Old Village House Door — Hok Tsui Tsuen —

A NEW Village Door — Shek O

312

Red Door — Ok tri Lam Village.

Moggie Door Stop —

Wong Chuk Hang.

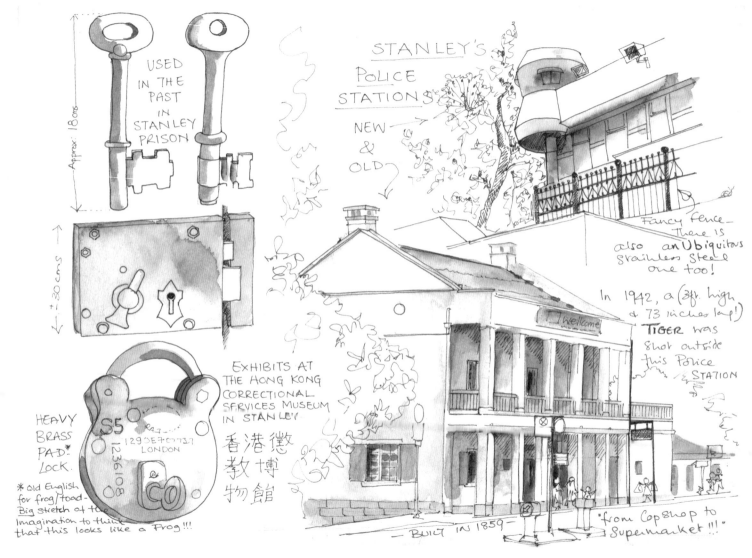

USED IN THE PAST IN STANLEY PRISON

Approx. 18 cms

± 30 cms

HEAVY BRASS PAD.* LOCK.

S5
129 DE刊○733
LONDON
1236108

* Old English for frog/toad — Big stretch of the Imagination to think that this looks like a Frog !!!

EXHIBITS AT THE HONG KONG CORRECTIONAL SERVICES MUSEUM IN STANLEY

香港懲
教博
物館

STANLEY'S POLICE STATIONS

NEW & OLD →

Fancy fence — There is also an Ubiquitous Srainless Steel one too!

In 1942, a (3ft. high & 73 inches long!) TIGER was shot outside this Police STATION

Welcome

— BUILT IN 1859 —

"from Cop shop to Supermarket !!!"

REDHILL PLAZA

海信

Smelly DURIAN

HAT SHOP IN STANLEY

Sketched by a dedicated Non-Shopper

SOUTHSIDE SHOPPING

南區 購物

— ABERDEEN —

HORIZON PLAZA —

SHEK O —

出價 ICE ICE

A MOTLEY CREW! An International grouping of
women DRAGON BOAT racers — from Australia, Holland, Switzerland,
LAMMA & one unidentified!

Two HOT Dudes

Pink Shiny hat

HI OFFSHORE WITHOUT A PADDLE

Lan Kwai Fong
蘭桂坊

SPECTATORS

... Or without a Dragon boat!

BRIGHT ORANGE

9am — High Tide

on Stanley Beach — lots of people and very hot sun

Two Cavemen — (Rather down in the mouth)

Typical Dimensions of a Hong Kong Dragon Boat—

Width: 3-3½ feet—
Length: 40 feet—
People: ± 22
+ 1 drum, 1 head + 1 tail — at least!!

Weight: Between 800 - 2000 lbs.

Heads are decorated on Race Day →

Ribbon

Individually fixed wooden 'beard'

Remarkable painted wooden head...

Hong Kong style

DRAGON BOAT
香港式龍舟

福綠不絕龍

METAL STUDS

One of four springs hidden inside the drum to give extra vibrancy.

FIXED HERE

X1·5

the Dragon Boat Drum —

STEERSMAN'S OAR

lost in the fray?

...and tail—

fixing pin

Traditional boats are made from Teak — Modern boats used throughout the world are made of fibreglass or Aluminium

In Action!

用力划!

At the Tip of Cape D'Aguilar — 鶴咀之端

Cape D'Aguilar Marine Reserve opened in July 1996 — Total Sea Area: 20 hectares (Fish, Hard & Soft coral, Gorgonian & Marine Invertebrates)

CAPE D'AGUILAR

KAU PEI CHAU

158

⊛ The Swire Institute of Marine Science, Department of Ecology & Biodiversity, HKU

Binocular Dissecting Microscope.

⊛ 22°13'N 114°15'E
Probably the Oldest Lighthouse on Hong Kong Island — Built in 1875 —

Marine Reserve — ABSOLUTELY! (NO FISHING! NOT EVEN FOR LUNCH!)

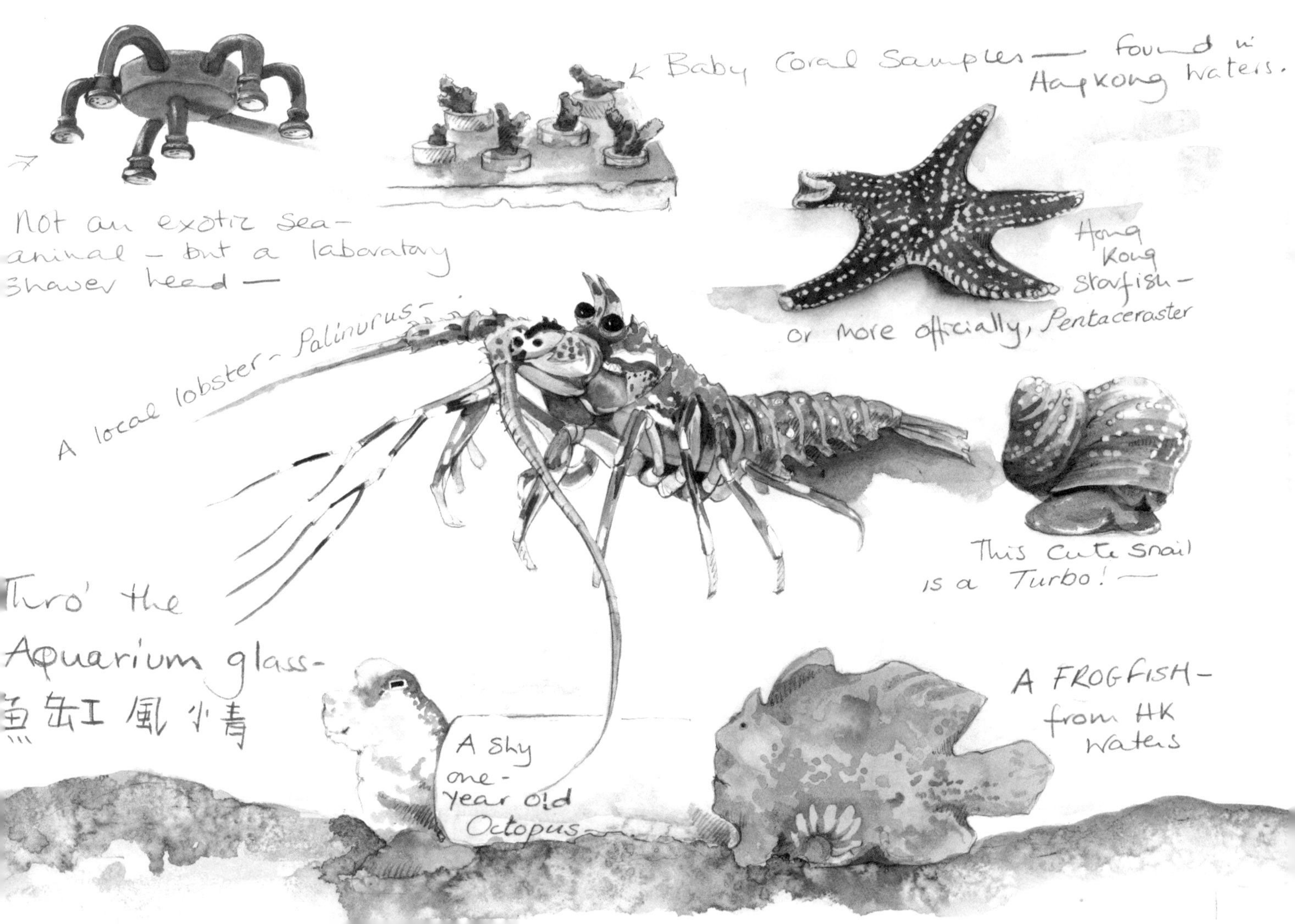

Not an exotic sea-animal — but a laboratory shower head —

k Baby Coral Samples — found in Hapkong waters.

Hong Kong Starfish — or more officially, Pentaceraster

A local lobster — Palinurus —

This cute snail is a Turbo! —

Tiro' the Aquarium glass— 魚缸風小青

A Shy one-year old Octopus —

A FROGFISH — from HK waters

HOK TSUI TSUEN
鶴咀村

Hok Tsui Tsuen means "Crane's Beak Village"

鶴咀村一號E

Address Ser
Stone!

There is also a ladder factory in this village →

Gossiping in the afternoon
午間閒談

This fort was built in ⑲ for protection in the event of Pirate raids —

Rows & rows of cotton gloves and shoes drying in the noonday Sun

樓梯物語……
ABOUT LADDERS_

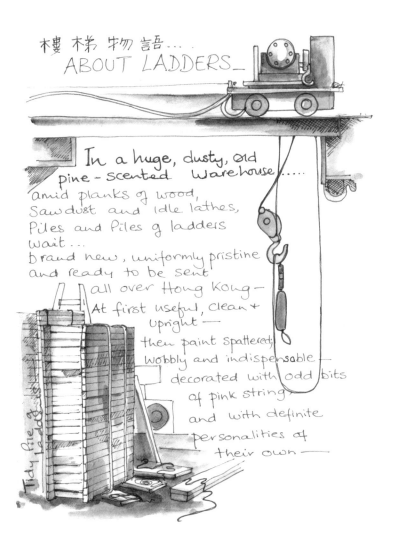

In a huge, dusty, old
pine-scented warehouse……
amid planks of wood,
sawdust and idle lathes,
piles and piles of ladders
wait…
brand new, uniformly pristine
and ready to be sent
all over Hong Kong—
At first useful, clean +
upright—
then paint splattered,
wobbly and indispensable—
decorated with odd bits
of pink string,
and with definite
personalities of
their own—

Tidy Pile of Ladders

STILL LIFE
"Domestica"

大潭
郊野公園
TAI TAM
COUNTRY PARK

TAI TAM
RESERVOIR

VICTORIA
GAP

TAI TAM INTERMEDIATE
RESERVOIR

TAI TAM
TUK RESERVOIR

CATCHWATER

TAI TAM
HARBOUR

It was a "big Spider" walk —
lots of them — minding their
own business in their own
suspension-webs*, hung over the
Catchwater —
A quiet walk — the kind where
big butterflies bump into you
and dragonflies hover by waterfalls,
...tiny crabs cross your path
and ants join
you for your picnic

Walking in Tai Tam Country Park
and along the Tai Tam East Catchwater

在大潭郊野公園里漫步

(* Arachnaduct, perhaps)

View across Tai
Tam Harbour —
大潭港對岸

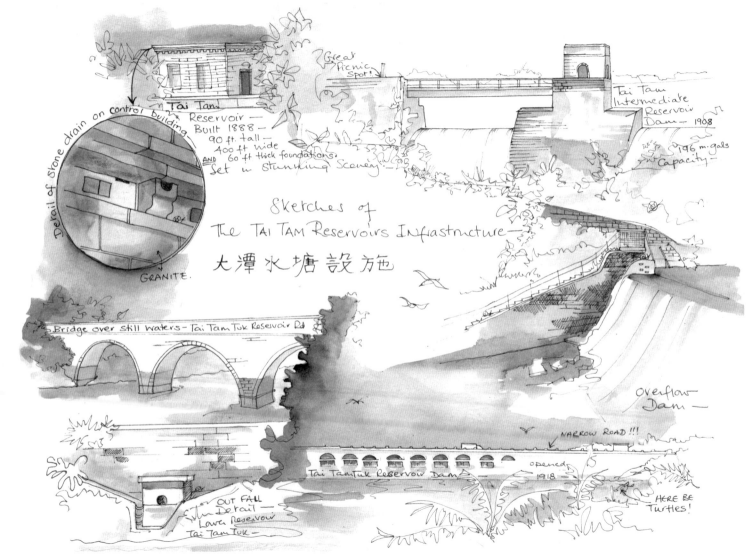

Detail of stone drain on control building

Tai Tam Reservoir — Built 1888 — 90 ft. tall — 400 ft wide AND 60 ft thick foundations. Set in stunning scenery —

Great Picnic Spot!

Tai Tam Intermediate Reservoir Dam — 1908

96 m. gals Capacity —

GRANITE.

Sketches of
The TAI TAM Reservoirs Infrastructure —
大潭水塘設施

Bridge over still waters — Tai Tam Tuk Reservoir Rd

Overflow Dam —

NARROW ROAD !!!

Tai Tam Tuk Reservoir Dam — Opened 1918

HERE BE TURTLES!

OUT FALL Detail Lower Reservoir Tai Tam Tuk

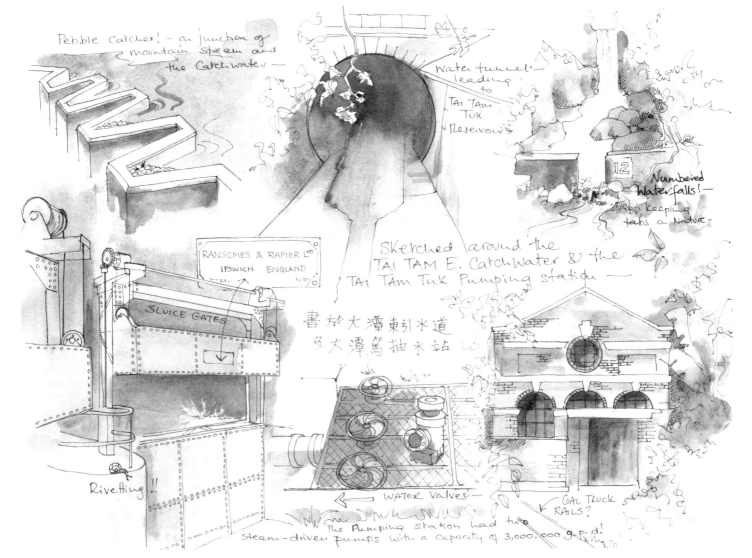

Pebble catcher! - a junction of mountain stream and the Catchwater -

Water tunnel leading to TAI TAM TUK Reservoir

Numbered Waterfalls! - keeping tabs on Nature -

12

RANSOMES & RAPIER L^D
IPSWICH ENGLAND

SLUICE GATES

Rivetting!!

Sketched around the TAI TAM E. Catchwater & the TAI TAM TUK Pumping station -

書於大潭東引水道
及大潭篤抽水站

WATER VALVES -

COAL TRUCK RAILS?

The Pumping station had two steam-driven pumps with a capacity of 3,000,000 g.p.d.!

大潭篤
TAI TAM TUK

A Village on the Shore of Tai Tam Harbour — A hidden place, seemingly forgotten .....
 Except for weekends when the whole area is a buzz with water sports enthusiasts.

JADE FLOWER

大章篤會
TAI TAM TUK SOCIETY
歡迎光臨
WELCOME

信箱

* A rather distressed Post !

Brick built towers in Tai Tam Harbour — Origin unknown — but suggestions range from Water Inflow, & Kiln to Ammunition Store (c 1890). x2
..... Any Ideas ??

Course Markers read for Dragon Boat Races —
(With numbers & Srebmun !)

-Boats in
Tai Tam
Harbour-

大潭港的
船隻

...like little
Toy boats!

32056 JAVA

大浪灣沙灘 ↑

"Surfies" chilling out—

Shades

A Plethora of flip-flopped feet ↑

8 surf boards and one inflatable 'gator—

SURF ANA

HB 租 Rent 2

Rock carvings

BIG WAVE BAY →

A sea of sun-brollies but not a big wave to be seen!

High over SHEK O — Actually too high to see properly!

ALL SHAPES & SIZES OF HIKERS —

Rock — Descent at Shek O —

Keep On Dreaming!

Determined & undaunted

Suave in Tai Tam.

Hiking with toddlers.

Under-dressed!

Overdressed?

"OTHER WAY MATE!"

ENERGETIC WEEKENDERS —
← AND ONE COUCH POTATO!

Taking care of his JET SKI to TEIWAN.

Surfing Dudes in SHEK O —

Wind Surfer — ST. STEPHEN'S BEACH.

Cyclist on Hong Kong Trail

Mini-Rugby at STANLEY FORT (FOR BLOKES OF ALL AGES!)

Looking across
the Tathong
Channel on a
very hot, very
calm day —
The Cape D'Aguilar
light house behind
+ Shek O in the
distance —

Anne's Garden —
Stick O —

Carolynne's
Roof top
garden —
STANLEY

— Gouache —

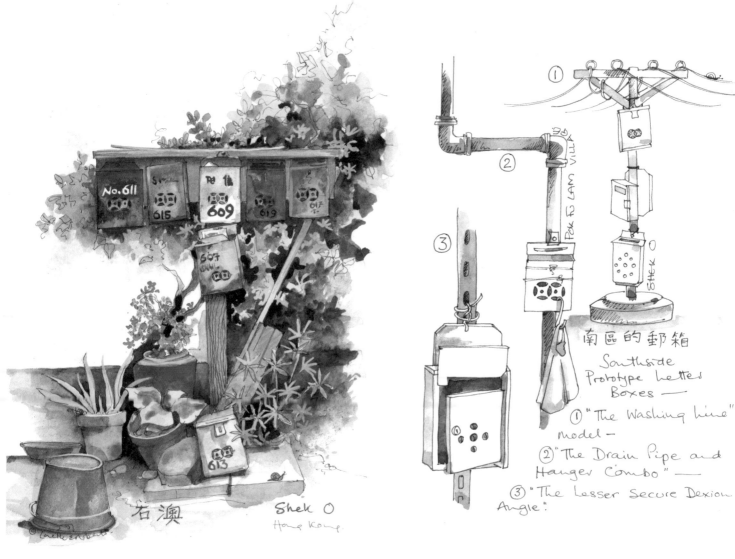

No.611

615

阿倫 609

619

607

613

右澳

Shek O
Hong Kong.

POK FU LAM VILLA

SHEK O

① ② ③

南區的郵箱

Southside
Prototype Letter
Boxes —

① "The Washing line"
Model —

② "The Drain Pipe and
Hanger Combo" —

③ "The Lesser Secure Dexion
Angle"

石澳
繽紛五彩小鎮

SHEK O —

Town of the Colourful
Houses —

SHEK-O BUS TERMINUS

Retro signage at the bus station —

"Auspicious Fragrant Pavilion" written in Xiao-Zhuan script —

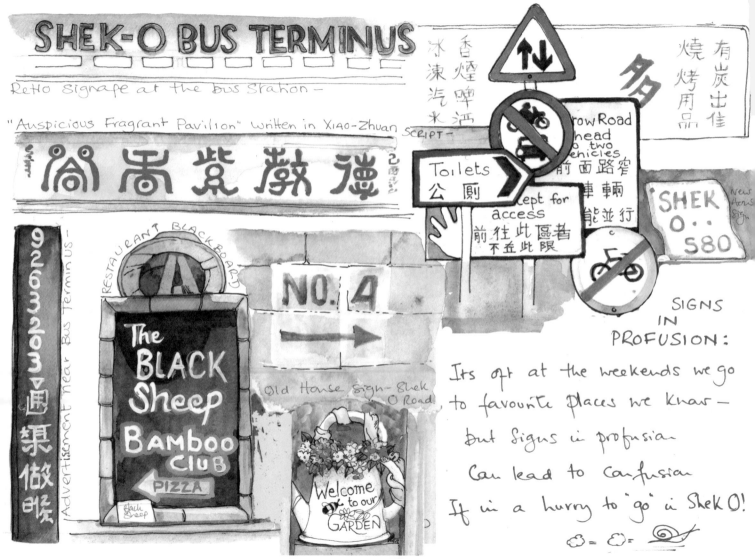

德馨紫香閣

冰凍啤酒汽水 香煙啤酒

多

有炭出佳 燒烤用品

↑↓

Narrow Road ahead to two vehicles
前面路窄
車輛
不能並行

Toilets
公厠

Except for access
前往此區者
不在此限

SHEK O·· S80
New Hous Sign

9263263 通渠做瞎

Advertisement near Bus Terminus —

RESTAURANT BLACKBOARD

A

NO. A →

The BLACK Sheep BAMBOO CLUB
PIZZA
Black Sheep

Old House Sign — Shek O Road

Welcome to our GARDEN

SIGNS IN PROFUSION:

Its oft at the weekends we go
to favourite places we know —
but signs in profusion
Can lead to confusion
If in a hurry to "go" in Shek O!

& finally....

you just never know whom
you will bump into in Southside
at the end of a long day!

最後..

在南區您將會
遇見意想不到
的情景